A TIMELINE OF

TANKS
AND OTHER
ARMORED
VEHICLES

by Tim Cooke

CAPSTONE PRESS
a capstone imprint

Edge Books are published by Capstone Press,
1710 Roe Crest Drive, North Mankato, Minnesota 56003
www.capstonepub.com

Published in 2018 by Capstone Publishing Ltd

Library of Congress Cataloging-in-Publication Data
Cataloging-in-publication information is on file with the Library of Congress.

ISBN: 978-1-5157-9195-9 (library binding)
ISBN: 978-1-5157-9201-7 (eBook PDF)

For Brown Bear Books Ltd:
Managing Editor: Tim Cooke
Designer: John Woolford
Editorial Director: Lindsey Lowe
Design Manager: Keith Davis
Children's Publisher: Anne O'Daly
Picture Manager: Sophie Mortimer
Production Director: Alastair Gourlay

Photo Credits
Front Cover: Bovingdon Tank Museum: bl; Patrice: cr; Thinkstock: Alexander Zam/istock tc;
United Kingdom Ministry of Defence: b.
Interior: Base Borden Military Museum: 18-19; Bovingdon Tank Museum: 14-15t; Bundeswehr: 24-25b, 28br;
D.Z. Guymed: 12-13; Department of Defense: 23tr, 24-25t, 24bc, 26-27t, 26bc, 27tr, 29tr; Imperial War Museum:
19tr; Israel Defense Forces: 29br; John Woolford: 1, 6-7, 9tr, 10-11b, 16-17, 20-21, 23br; Library of Congress: 5cr,
22bc; Ministry of Defense Norway: 25tr; National Archives: 20br; Patrice: 22-23; Robert Hunt Library: 5tr, 5bl, 6bc,
7cr, 7bc, 8-9b, 9br, 10bc, 11tr, 13tr, 13bc, 14-15b, 15cr, 16bc, 17tr, 17br, 18bc, 19bc, 21tr. Russian Defense Ministry:
26-27b; Shutterstock: M. Dogan 10-11t, Everett Historical 12br; Thinkstock: iStock 4-5, 8-9t; United Kingdom
Ministry of Defence: 28-29. Artistic effects: Shutterstock

Brown Bear Books has made every attempt to contact the copyright holders.
If you have any information please contact licensing@brownbearbooks.co.uk

Printed in the USA
5607/AG/17

TABLE OF CONTENTS

ARMORED VEHICLES

Tanks and armored vehicles have been an important part of warfare for more than 100 years. Since tanks first appeared in World War I (1914–1918), engineers have figured out ways to make them more powerful, and military leaders have found different ways to use them in battle.

The creation of the tank brought together a range of different technologies. The gas engine had been invented in 1876. Small, powerful artillery weapons became more advanced throughout the 1800s. Advancements in armor had been developed over hundreds of years.

ARMORED KNIGHTS

From around 600 to 850, soldiers went into battle protected by thick leather aprons and jackets. Later, they began to wear chain mail, which was made from fastening together links of steel into a shirt. Eventually, mounted soldiers called knights began wearing full suits of steel armor. A separate piece of armor covered each part of the body, allowing the knight to move freely.

THE FIRST TANK

More than 500 years ago, Italian artist Leonardo da Vinci designed the first tank. He drew a wheeled wooden vehicle. Soldiers inside would fire out through holes. Da Vinci's design was inspired by the shape of a turtle's shell. However, the vehicle was never built, and it remained just an idea.

IRONCLADS

Armored vehicles were developed in the mid-1800s. Navies began to protect warships with iron plates. During the American Civil War (1861–1865), a battle took place between two ironclad ships, the *Monitor* and the *Merrimack*.

TRACKED VEHICLES

The first tracked vehicles were developed in the early 1900s. The idea of using continuous tracks originally came from agriculture. Tractor wheels often sank into soft ground. Tracks helped spread the vehicle's weight evenly, allowing it to pass over soft ground.

THE FIRST ARMORED CARS

At the start of World War I, the British came up with the idea of using cars on the front lines. The cars were used to carry out patrols.

The Rolls Royce Silver Ghost was one of the most expensive cars of the time. When war broke out in 1914, Rolls Royce owners gave their cars to the British Army for war use. The cars were covered in steel amor and fitted with a machine gun. The army used 72 Rolls Royces during the conflict. On the Western Front in France, the cars often became stuck in the muddy ground. They were most useful in the flat, open deserts of the Middle East.

THE TURRET of the armored Rolls Royce allowed a standing soldier to fire the machine gun.

TIMELINE

1904
ON THE FARM
David Roberts invents a continuous track to use in place of wheels on farm tractors. In 1907 he demonstrates the track to the British Army.

1907
NEW TREADS
Californian Benjamin Holt patents the first practical tractor with "crawler type" tracks. These vehicles are used for farming and logging.

SPECIFICATIONS

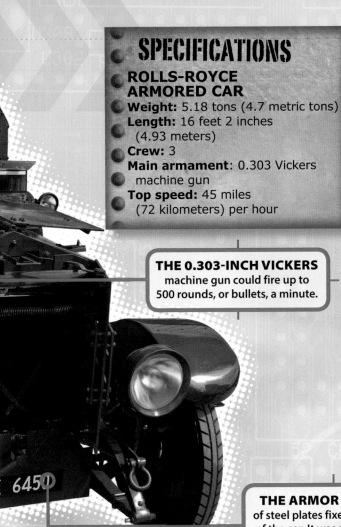

ROLLS-ROYCE ARMORED CAR
Weight: 5.18 tons (4.7 metric tons)
Length: 16 feet 2 inches
(4.93 meters)
Crew: 3
Main armament: 0.303 Vickers
machine gun
Top speed: 45 miles
(72 kilometers) per hour

THE 0.303-INCH VICKERS machine gun could fire up to 500 rounds, or bullets, a minute.

THE ARMOR was made up of steel plates fixed to the frame of the car. It was nearly 0.5 inch (12 millimeters) thick.

645

POWER PEOPLE

LAWRENCE OF ARABIA
The British Army officer T. E. Lawrence was known as Lawrence of Arabia. In World War I, he fought with rebels from Arabia fighting against their Turkish rulers. He used nine armored Rolls Royces in the desert. He said the cars were "more valuable than rubies."

1914

PULLING POWER
At the start of World War I, some Holt tractors were used instead of horses to carry weapons and supplies to the front lines.

1915

ROLLS ROYCE
The British Army begins to use Rolls Royce armored cars. The cars were not suited to the muddy conditions in France, but were more useful in the desert.

THE FIRST TANKS

The British invented the first tanks during World War I. In France, the Western Front had become a sea of mud. The army needed a vehicle that could cross the soft ground.

The British army secretly developed what they called "land ships." The vehicles had tracks instead of wheels. This meant they could cross muddy ground without getting stuck. They could also break through barbed wire. The **protoype**, "Little Willie," looked like a large tank for holding water. The name stuck. The British used this tank, the Mark I, in battle for the first time in 1916. It had machine guns mounted on its sides.

> **THERE WAS NO TURRET** in order to keep the tank's center of gravity low. This made it more stable.

> **THE SLOPING TRACKS** made it easier for the Mark I to climb obstacles. The tank was long enough to cross any trench.

TIMELINE

1915
KILLEN-STRAIT
The U.S. engineering firm Killen-Strait invents a tracked tractor. It has one track at the front, and two behind.

1915
LITTLE WILLIE
The British Army makes the Mark I, nicknamed "Little Willie." They hope to use the new vehicles to break through German lines on the Western Front.

1916
BIG WILLIE
The British introduce an improved tank, "Big Willie." It is shaped as a **rhombus**. The shape makes its tracks longer, and makes it better for crossing trenches.

MARK I TANK
Weight: 28.4 tons
(25.7 metric tons)
Length: 26 feet (7.92 meters)
Crew: 8
Main armament: 5 x 0.303 inches
machine guns
Top speed: 3.7 miles
(5.9 kilometers) per hour

INSIDE OUT

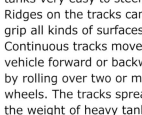

CONTINUOUS TRACKS
Having tracks makes tanks very easy to steer. Ridges on the tracks can grip all kinds of surfaces. Continuous tracks move a vehicle forward or backward by rolling over two or more wheels. The tracks spread the weight of heavy tanks, preventing them from sinking in soft ground.

THE SIDE BULGES
carried machine guns or a longer, heavy gun.

1916

INTO ACTION
On September 15, the British use the Mark I for the first time during the Battle of the Somme. Around 40 tanks advance 1 mile (1.6 km) into German territory.

prototype—the first version of a new invention from which other versions are developed
rhombus—a four-sided shape in which all four sides are the same length

A NEW DESIGN

After the success of British tanks in 1916, the French built their own tanks. The car maker Renault came up with a smaller, lighter design for a tank.

Renault worked with the French army. The army decided that it would prefer to have a larger number of lighter tanks than a few heavy tanks. In 1917 Renault began to produce the FT-17. When the United States entered World War I in April 1917, the U.S. Army had no tanks of its own. It arranged with the French to use the FT-17. The tanks went into action for the first time in May 1918. They used a tactic called "swarming," in which many FT-17s worked together to overwhelm enemy defenses. Because it operated in swarms, the tank was nicknamed "The Mosquito."

THE HATCH could be opened when the tank was not in action to allow the driver to see where he was going.

TIMELINE

1917

THE MOSQUITO

The French launch the Renault FT-17, the first modern tank. Its design is still in use. It has a front driver and central fighting compartment with a revolving turret.

1917

FIRST TANK BATTLE

On November 20, at Cambrai, in France, the British Army use Mark IV tanks to break down barbed wire defenses and cross German trenches.

SPECIFICATIONS

RENAULT FT-17 TANK
Weight: 7.2 tons (6.5 metric tons)
Length: 16 feet 5 inches (5 meters)
Crew: 2
Main armament: 37 mm gun
Top speed: 5 miles (7.7 kilometers) per hour

INSIDE OUT

THE TANK COMMANDER sat in the revolving turret. He also fired the machine gun or cannon.

STANDARD LAYOUT

The FT-17 set the pattern for nearly all later tanks. Its main gun was held in a rotating turret on top of the vehicle. The engine was in a compartment at the back of the vehicle. The compartment for the crew was at the front. Renault produced nearly 3,000 FT-17s during the war.

THE ROUNDED BACK helped the tracks get a grip to climb out of any trenches the tank might fall into.

1919

ARMORED FUTURE

Major J.F.C. Fuller plans to arm the British Army with tank units.

1920

US DECISION

The U.S. Army makes the Tank Corps part of the **Infantry** division rather than the **Cavalry** division. The Infantry prefer the development of heavier, slower tanks.

infantry—soldiers who fight on foot
cavalry—soldiers who fight on horseback

THE MECHANICAL CAVALRY

After World War I, military engineers developed new types of tank. They hoped fast armored vehicles would replace traditional cavalry regiments.

The Versailles Peace Treaty of 1919 demanded Germany stop making weapons. When Adolf Hitler came to power in 1933, he ignored the treaty and ordered the army to develop tanks. The Germans built the Panzer I in 1934. Panzer was short for *Panzerkampfwagen*, which is German for "armored fighting vehicle." It was a fast, light tank intended to be used against enemy infantry.

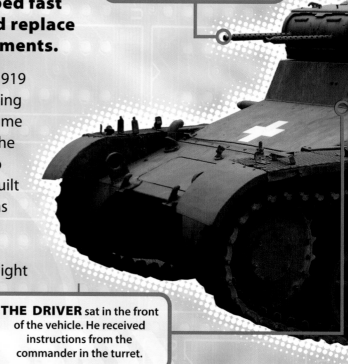

THE ROTATING TURRET held two MG-13 machine guns. The guns were effective against infantry but were not effective against other tanks.

THE DRIVER sat in the front of the vehicle. He received instructions from the commander in the turret.

TIMELINE

1928
JOINT FORCE
The United States brings together all branches of the Army to cooperate in an experimental mechanized force.

1933
HITLER REARMS
Adolf Hitler, the new German leader, orders tanks to be developed in secret. This breaks the Treaty of Versailles, which forbade Germany to rearm after World War I.

SPECIFICATIONS

PANZER MK I
Weight: 6 tons (5.4 metric tons)
Length: 13.2 feet (4.02 meters)
Crew: 2
Main armament: two 7.92 mm
MG13 machine guns
Top speed: 23 miles
(37 kilometers) per hour off-road

POWER PEOPLE

GEORGE PATTON

George Patton commanded U.S. tanks in World War I. After the war, he argued for the creation of a special tank **corps**. He believed that tanks could be used for rapid advances into enemy territory. Patton became a leading general in World War II (1939–1945).

> **THE ORIGINAL ARMOR**
> was only 0.5 inch (13 mm) thick.
> It was later strengthened.

1934

FIRST PANZER

Germany builds the Panzer I, with light armor and two machine guns. Intended for training purposes, it stays in service until 1945.

1935

TEMPORARY TANK

Germany introduces the Panzer II. It is only meant to fill in until the Panzer III and IV are ready for action. Instead, it is used to invade Poland in 1939.

corps—a large section of an army on the battlefield

BLITZKRIEG!

At the start of World War II, Germany used a new tactic called *Blitzkrieg*, which is German for "lightning war." It was based on using tanks.

Light tank units raced into enemy territory, supported by fighter aircraft and bombers. The most important tank in the Blitzkrieg was the Panzer IV. It had stronger armor and a more powerful gun than the earlier Panzers. It was designed to be able to destroy enemy anti-tank guns and defensive positions. In the first months of World War II, the Germans easily overran Poland, Belgium, and France because of the speed of their **mechanized** attack.

THE TURRET held the tank commander, the gunner, and the gun loader.

TIMELINE

1939

GLOBAL WAR
World War II begins. It is the first conflict in which tanks play a key role.

1939

BLITZKRIEG!
Germany begins the war by launching a Blitzkrieg against Poland on September 1. German tanks led the invasion, which defeated Poland in just over a month.

SPECIFICATIONS

PANZER IV
Weight: 27.6 tons (25 metric tons)
Length: 19 feet 5 inches (5.92 meters)
Crew: 5
Main armament: 7.5-cm KwK 40
Top speed: 16 miles (25 kilometers) per hour off-road

POWER PEOPLE

HEINZ GUDERIAN

General Heinz Guderian came up with the Blitzkrieg tactic. He said that tanks should keep moving through enemy territory. That way the enemy never had a chance to fight back.

THE DRIVER and radio operator sat at the front of the tank. In action, the radio operator also acted as a machine gunner.

1940
WAR IN THE WEST
In May, German tanks lead the Blitzkrieg into Belgium, the Netherlands, Luxembourg, and France. They are victorious in around six weeks.

1940
VICTORY PARADE
On June 14, German tanks and infantry parade past the Arc de Triomphe in Paris to celebrated the surrender of France.

mechanize—to use machines to perform a task

PLAINS AND DESERTS

During World War II, fighting spread to North Africa and Russia. The North African deserts and the flat Russian plains were ideal for tank warfare.

THE TURRET was large enough for five men to work inside the tank. All the crew had different tasks.

The Germans had thousands of quick Panzer III tanks supported by thousands of heavier Panzer IVs. The Germans believed these tanks were better protected and had more powerful guns than any enemy tanks. However, they did not know about a new Soviet tank, the T-34. Cheap to make and reliable, the T-34 had thick, sloping armor that protected it from enemy shells. When the Germans invaded the Soviet Union in June 1941, T-34s destroyed many Panzers.

TIMELINE

1940
SOVIET MODEL
The Russian T-34 goes into production. It has sloped armor and is easy to steer and control. It is quick and cheap to manufacture in large numbers.

1941
BARBAROSSA
In June the Germans invade the Soviet Union. Many Panzer IIIs and IVs are destroyed by Russian T-34s, which have strong armor and more powerful guns.

SPECIFICATIONS

T-34

Weight: 30.9 metric tons (28 tonnes)

Length: 27 feet 11 inches (8.15 meters)

Crew: 5

Main armament: 85-mm ZiS-S-53 tank gun

Top speed: 32 miles (51 kilometers) per hour

IN ACTION

THE MAIN ARMAMENT was originally a 76.2 mm gun. It was replaced in late 1943 by a more powerful 85-mm gun.

BATTLE OF KURSK

The biggest tank battle of the war took place in the summer of 1943. In the east, the Soviets had halted the German invasion. They were pushing the Germans back out of Russia. The two sides met in a tank battle at Kursk. Nearly 3,000 German tanks failed to break through the front line of the Soviets, who had more than 5,000 tanks.

THE TRACKS of the T-34 did not often break or come loose. The tank was so reliable it was still used in 27 countries in the 1990s.

1941

M4 SHERMAN

The U.S. Army begins to build the M4 Sherman tank. Nearly 50,000 M4s are built during the war.

1942

MOST FEARED

Germany develops the 60-ton Tiger tank in answer to the T-34. It is the most feared World War II tank, but does not work well on the frozen ground of the Eastern Front.

THE ADAPTABLE TANK

During World War II, tanks were adapted for specialized roles. They were used to lay temporary bridges across rivers, to clear minefields, or to carry weapons such as flamethrowers.

The Americans and British **modified** existing tanks to perform specific tasks. The new vehicles looked strange, so soldiers called them "funnies." One of the most common adaptations was the American M4 Sherman Crab. The tank was fitted with an arm called a flail. It held heavy, spinning chains. The flail was used to clear minefields. The spinning chains made the mines explode, while the crew inside the tank were protected by heavy armor.

THE MAIN GUN was supplemented by a smaller machine gun fired by the tank's copilot.

THE FLAIL ARM could be raised to allow the tank to use its gun in combat. The arm had heavy protective armor.

TIMELINE

1943
KURSK
The largest tank battle in history takes place on the Eastern Front at Kursk between July and August. The Soviets win a decisive victory over the Germans.

1944
SUPER TANK
Germany develops the super-heavy Panzer VIII or Maus. Only one is ever completed. It is the heaviest enclosed armored fighting vehicle ever built.

M4 SHERMAN CRAB
Weight: 33.4 tons (30.3 metric tons)
Length: 19 feet 2 inches (6.6 meters)
Crew: 5
Main armament: 75-mm gun
Top speed: 30 miles (48 kilometers)
 per hour

INSIDE OUT

SUPPORTING D-DAY

On D-Day, June 6, 1944, dozens of specially adapted "funnies" were used in the Allied invasion of France. They included Sherman DDs, which had waterproof screens so they could "swim" ashore through deep water. Other funnies included road-laying and bridge-laying tanks.

THE FLAIL on the Sherman Crab was made from heavy chains with steel balls at the end of them. The chains rotated and hit the ground to detonate mines just beneath.

1944

D-DAY
On June 6 dozens of specially adapted tanks go ashore with Allied landing forces on the beaches of northern France.

1944

TANK CHARGE
In July the British launch Operation Goodwood during the Battle for Caen, Normandy. Around 1,100 British tanks defeat 377 German tanks.

modify—to change something for a specific purpose

ARMORED CARS

In World War II fighting took place over wide areas. It was important for soldiers to be able to cover great distances quickly to check on enemy positions. There was always a risk that they would meet enemy forces.

Armies built armored cars, such as the U.S. M8, which the British called the Greyhound. Armored cars were quicker and lighter than tanks. They traveled ahead of tank columns to locate enemy positions. The M8 carried a long-distance radio to report whatever it found to army commanders back at base. The M8 was heavily armed with a main gun and a machine gun. That meant the vehicle could fight its way out of trouble if it ran into enemy forces.

LONG-RANGE RADIO sent information about the enemy to headquarters, making the M8 the "eyes and ears" of the U.S. Army.

TIMELINE

1945

END OF THE WAR
World War II ends in Europe in April. Britain has 30,000 tanks in service. The United States has 90,000, the Soviet Union 105,000, and Germany 62,000.

1950

KOREAN WAR (1950–1953)
American M46 Patton tanks fight against North Korean T-34s. Despite the use of jets, the war was mainly fought on the ground.

M8 "Greyhound"
Weight: 8.6 tons (7.8 metric tons)
Length: 16 feet 5 inches
(5 meters)
Crew: 4
Main armament: 37-mm M6 gun
Top speed: 55 miles
(89 kilometers) per hour

EYEWITNESS

SHELLS for the 37-mm gun are stored in racks inside the turret.

" The Army's latest combat vehicle is a six-wheeled, eight-ton armored job that can hit high speed over practically any type of **terrain**....
The M8 carries a crew of four and it is primarily for use in **reconnaissance** and combat. "

Yank, *a magazine for U.S. military personnel, reviews the M8, June 23, 1944*

SIX WHEELS with rugged tires enabled the vehicle to move quickly over smooth ground.

1952

WATER VEHICLE
The Soviet Union builds PT76 light tanks. They are the first **amphibious** vehicles to use jets of water to push them through the water.

1960

M113
The M113 Advanced Personnel Carrier (APC) enters service. It is the most widely used armored vehicle in the Vietnam War (1955–1971).

terrain—the physical features of a piece of land
reconnaissance—the military observation of a region in order to locate enemy positions
amphibious—able to operate in water and on land

ADVANCED PERSONNEL CARRIERS

The U.S. M113 APC was introduced in the 1960s. It has served in every conflict since the Vietnam War.

The M113 was designed to move small units of infantry into position on the battlefield. It has been in service for more than 50 years. The M113 is the most widely used of all APCs. It was developed to be light enough to transport into combat zones by airplane. The M113's armor is made from aluminum, which is a light metal. The vehicle can carry up to 11 armed soldiers into a battle zone.

> **THE MAIN GUN** is a 0.50 mm machine gun. Anti-tank missiles can also be fitted to the vehicle.

> **THE 38-MM ALUMINUM** armor is light, but offers the same high degree of protection as steel.

TIMELINE

1965

M113
U.S. troops land in Vietnam to fight the North Vietnamese. The M113 is used to move soldiers around Vietnam.

1965

NO TURRET
The Swedish Stridsvagn 103 is the first tank to be powered by a gas turbine. The tank's design is unusual, because it has no turret.

SPECIFICATIONS

M113

Weight: 13.6 tons (12.3 metric tons)
Length: 15 feet 11 inches
 (4.86 meters)
Crew: 2 + 11 passengers
Main armament: M2 Browning
 machine gun
Top speed: 42 miles (67.6 kilometers)
 per hour

EYEWITNESS

" I saw the red flash of the round and the burst of smoke on the side of the vehicle as the round penetrated the side armor. The round penetrated into the interior of the vehicle and hit an anti-tank weapon setting it off, killing one man and wounding several others. "

Patrick Haygood,
24th U.S. Infantry Division,
Gulf War, 1991

62.375

FLAPS ON THE TRACKS make the M113 amphibious. When it is in water, the flaps push it along.

1967

THE SIX-DAY WAR

War in the Middle East sees 1,000 Israeli tanks fight and defeat 2,050 Egyptian, Jordanian, and Syrian tanks.

1970

LEOPARD

West Germany begins to develop the Leopard MBT tank. Its design is so successful that the Germans export it around the world.

MAIN BATTLE TANKS

Since World War II tanks have become more powerful. The heaviest tanks are main battle tanks (MBTs). They lack speed but have powerful weapons. In battle, they are supported by quicker light tanks.

The Abrams M1 is the MBT of the U.S. Army and the U.S. Marine Corps. The Abrams entered service in 1980. It has also been sold to many other armies. The tank can operate in any weather, in the daytime or at night. The Abrams is extremely powerful. Its main gun can destroy any other armored fighting vehicle in the world.

MAIN GUN fires 120-mm caliber shells. It fires different types of shells according to the target.

SLOPING HULL helps deflect enemy shells, preventing them from piercing the armor.

TIMELINE

1980

MAIN BATTLE TANK

The M1 Abrams Main Battle Tank goes into production. It has new armor made from layers of plastics and **ceramics**.

1982

NEW GENERATION

The Germans introduce the Leopard 2 MBT. The Leopard is first used during a peacekeeping mission in Kosovo.

SPECIFICATIONS

Abrams M1
Weight: 68.5 tons (62 metric tons)
Length: 32 feet (9.77 meters)
Crew: 4
Main armament: 120-mm cannon
Top speed: 42 miles
   (67.5 kilometers) per hour

INSIDE OUT

NEW MATERIALS

The Abrams used a lighter form of armor to protect them from armor-piercing missiles. Scientists developed armor made from layers of ceramic and **polymer**. As well as weighing less, these new materials offer better protection against modern bullets and missiles.

CATERPILLAR
tracks are partly protected by the tank's side armor.

1984

HMMWV
The High Mobility Multi-Purpose Wheeled Vehicle, or Humvee, goes into production. It is a development of the wartime jeep.

1988

BRITISH WARRIOR
The British Army introduces the Warrior infantry fighting vehicle. It provides support and back-up to Britain's main battle tanks.

ceramic—made of clay that has been hardened by heat to make it stronger
polymer—an artificial material such as plastic or resin that is created using chemicals

25

ARMORED FIGHTING VEHICLES

A new type of fighting vehicle was built in the 1990s: infantry fighting vehicles (IFVs). They included the U.S. M2 and M3 Bradley.

The IFVs were a development of earlier armored cars. They were designed to act as motorized cavalry. They accompanied columns of tanks or protected infantry as they advanced. In the First Gulf War (1990–1991), the M2 Bradley carried out patrols in the desert to monitor enemy movements. The 25-mm gun could destroy enemy armored vehicles or airplanes. The IFVs were also fast enough to move quickly away from danger.

TROOP COMPARTMENT carries two fully equipped soldiers.

TIMELINE

1991

PERSIAN GULF
Coalition forces fighting the Iraqis in Kuwait use Abrams M1 tanks and Bradley M3 Armored Fighting Vehicles to destroy Iraqi armored vehicles.

1998

NEW CHALLENGER
The British introduce the highly advanced Challenger 2. It gains a reputation for being the most reliable MBT in the world.

SPECIFICATIONS

M3 Bradley
Weight: 25 tons (23 metric tons)
Length: 21.2 feet (6.45 meters)
Crew: 3 + 2 passengers
Main armament: 25-mm M242 chain gun
Top speed: 35–41 miles (56–66 kilometers) per hour

IN ACTION

25 MM MAIN GUN is powerful enough to destroy virtually any enemy tank.

FIRST GULF WAR
During the First Gulf War, the M2 Bradley destroyed more Iraqi armored vehicles than the M1 Abrams battle tank. Although the Bradley was not as heavily armored as the M1 Abrams, the Iraqis only managed to destroy three Bradleys.

BRADLEY M3 CAMOUFLAGE comes in four different colors, to match different terrains — sand, woodland, olive drab, and "urban."

2015
NEXT GENERATION
The Russians start production of the T-14 Armata. It is the next generation of MBT. The T-14's turret is controlled remotely by soldiers inside the main tank.

2017
WORLD'S BEST
The German Leopard 2A7 is the world's most powerful and best-defended tank. It has **composite** armor made from new ceramics, titanium, and steel.

composite—describes a material that is made up from a number of different materials

NEW GENERATION

In wars in Afghanistan and Iraq, roadside bombs and suicide bombings have changed the nature of warfare. Armored vehicles have changed to protect soldiers.

New tanks have bomb-resistant side armor and added protection on their undersides to protect against bomb blasts. The tank body is higher off the ground, which is designed to lessen the impact of a blast. Inside, the crew have special seats protected by iron plates. They wear harnesses so they do not get thrown around if the tank is hit by a bomb blast.

EIGHT PERISCOPES give the commander 360-degree vision. Thermal imaging is used for night vision.

THE HIGH PROTECTION ARMOR of the Challenger 2 is twice as strong as the armor on older tanks.

INTO THE FUTURE

TOMORROW'S TANKS
A number of countries are developing MBTs. Some of the new tanks are updated versions of current tanks. Others are brand new. These tanks have strong composite armor for protection. They have modern remote-control firing systems. The operator uses a screen to control the turret, main gun, and machine guns from inside the tank.

SPECIFICATIONS

Challenger 2
Weight: 82.7 tons (75 metric tons)
Length: 27 feet 3 inches (8.3 meters)
Crew: 4
Main armament: L30 A1 120-mm
  rifled gun
Speed: 37 miles (59 kilometers)
  per hour, on road

INSIDE OUT

COMPUTER CONTROL

Today, computers control a tank's main guns. This means that a gun can still hit its target even if the tank is traveling over bumpy ground. The computer tracks and updates the target's location. It uses the relative speed of the two tanks to calculate where to aim its guns in order to hit the enemy tank.

CHALLENGER 2 has a rifled gun with grooves on the inside of the barrel. This spins the shells as they fly through the air. Spinning makes them fly straighter toward their target.

NEW MBTS

The next generation of MBTs include the German Leopard 2 (left) and the Israeli Mekava 4 Windbreaker (right).

periscope—a tube with mirrors for viewing objects on a higher level than the observer

GLOSSARY

amphibious (am-FIB-ee-us)—able to operate in water and on land

cavalry (CAV-uhl-ree)—soldiers who fight on horseback

ceramic (sir-AM-ik)—made of clay that has been permanently hardened by heat to make it stronger

composite (kuhm-PAH-zuht)—describes a material that is made up from a number of different materials

corps (CORE)—a large section of an army on the battlefield

infantry (in-FUN-tree)—soldiers who fight on foot

mechanize (MEK-an-ize)—to use machines to perform a task

modify (MOD-uh-fy)—to change something for a specific purpose

periscope (PARE-uh-scope)—a tube with mirrors for viewing objects on a higher level than the observer

polymer (pol-EE-mur)—an artificial material such as plastic or resin that is created using chemicals

prototype (pro-toh-TIPE)—the first version of a new invention from which other versions are developed

reconnaissance (ruh-KON-uh-senz)—the military observation of a region in order to locate enemy positions and learn enemy plans

rhombus (ROM-bus)—a four-sided shape in which all four sides are the same length

terrain (tuh-RAIN)—the physical features of a piece of land

READ MORE

Colson, Rob. *Tanks and Military Vehicles*. Ultimate Military Machines. New York: PowerKids Press, 2013.

Kiland, Taylor Baldwin, and Gerry Souter. *Armored Tanks*. Military Engineering in Action. New York: Enslow Publishing, 2015.

Mavrikis, Peter. *What's Inside Tanks?* What's Inside? New York: PowerKids Press, 2016.

INTERNET SITES

Use FactHound to find Internet sites related to this book.

Visit www.facthound.com

Just type in 9781515791959 and go.

Check out projects, games and lots more at
www.capstonekids.com

INDEX